Sunny With A Chance Of Rain

By Honey Thomas

Sunny With A Chance Of Rain

Copyright© 2021 Honey Thomas

All rights reserved. Printed in the United States of America.

No part of this book may be used or reproduced in any manner whatsoever without written permission except in the case of brief quotations embodied in critical articles and reviews.

ISBN:

ISBN-13: 978-1-7355974-3-0

I dedicate this book to myself. I deserve it.

Disclaimer: POSSIBLE TRIGGERS...

This book is written from experience, be it directly or indirectly. I can only speak from my point of view on these matters of life. People, places, and things that have affected me in some shape, form, or fashion. I've decided to chat about it.

Hey, I'm just talking about what I'm talking about.

I hope it helps you to overcome obstacles, a troubled past, a hindering present, bad relationships, past hurts, and angers. My hope is that it brings out the survivor in you, and you embrace the beautiful, wonderful, brave and strong person that you are. Love on yourself.

Much Love,
Honey

Table of Contents

1. Nobody Said It Would Be Easy
2. March To The Beat Of The Drum That Nobody Else Can Catch The Groove To
3. Don't Let Your Past Make Your Present Trash
4. You Are Appreciated
5. Girl, They Are Going To Get WTF You Have To Give
6. Everywhere You Turn There You Are (Encourage Yourself)
7. Dock Your Ships When They No Longer Flow With Your Waves (Relation-Ships, Friend-Ships, Family-Ships and Situation-Ships)
8. To Be The Best Version Of Yourself, You Have To Choose Yourself
9. Don't Dismiss My Feelings
10. 4-6-89…6:02am
11. Tell Somebody
12. Confirmation
13. That's The Way I Feel About Cha
14. Issues
15. Love Won't Let Me Wait
16. Be Quiet, Be Still
17. Hell-Yeah, I'm Mad
18. Honey
19. The Good, The Bad, The Ugly

20. Remodel and Rebuild

21. Sun Rain Down On Me

22. Write The Vision, Make It Plain

23. Self-Compassion

24. Black Lotus Flower

25. Sunny With A Chance Of Rain

Nobody Said It Would Be Easy

Laugh now and cry later. Cry now and laugh later. No matter which way it goes, in life, we all laugh and cry sometimes.

Over the years I have cried for many reasons. Deaths, births, relationships and that one time I hit my shin on the edge of the metal bed post when I was 11 years old…ouch.

At a young age I learned to suffer in silence. That is one of the worst vices I could have picked up.

It's unfortunate that we're not given a map on life that we can follow to the letter and maneuver effortlessly down the expressway in the middle lane…not to fast and not to slow, but at a steady pace.

Nobody said life would be easy…but dammit it should be. Raise your hand if you asked to be here. Just as I thought, not one of us. However, we were thrown into this off-kilter melting pot and left to figure things out on our own. Most will say, "It's a blessing to be here." Yeah well, how can you be happy about something you never knew about in the first place. Still and all, I'm glad to be here for some of the experiences I've encountered and quite enjoyed.

Which brings me to my next point of nobody said it would be easy. The bad experiences one encounters in life is traumatizing for most, debilitating even. Some use it as a crutch, and some use it as fuel to be the best version of themselves. Either way it's yours to do with it what you will. You come alive at your own pace and move on your own behalf. When you see fit to do so. Don't let anyone or anything stop you from your destiny. STOP SUFFERING IN SILENCE and speak your truth. Use some curse words too for a grand effect!

March To The Beat Of The Drum That Nobody Else Can Catch The Groove To

5,6,5 6 7 8…

Get into formation…your own formation. Be your own organic, authentic self. Live your life the way you chose too. For far to long you've been in sync with the wrong people. Being led down a life of nothingness. Deceit, dead ends, lies, empty promises, generational curses, this the way my mama did it so, this is the way I know. If it's not broke don't fix it.

 Bullshit!

Just because that's the way you were taught when you were 3 years old, doesn't mean that's the end all way of life. As we get older, we must find ways to make life work for us, and not just blindly work for life…please read that part again.

By no means am I saying throw your entire upbringing away. (Well, some people may have too, but that's a story for another day).

What I'm saying is, keep the best advice you were given as a child, teen, young adult, and add some new words to it. Add some new spicy music. Once you catch the rhythm of the drum, and you began to feel strong enough to step out on faith, loud enough to speak your peace, sharp enough to command attention and direct people to get on your bandwagon or catch the next one… Because you're taking off with or without them.

Yesss, can you feel it? Are your feet tap'n? Is your head bop'n? Are your shoulders lean'n? Don't look around ashamed, worried about who see's you dancing with no music playing. This is about you, not them. Now they want to dance to the beat of your drum because they see the new and improved you. Grooving and living your best life, emotionally, mentally, physically, spiritually, and financially stable. You just stepped into your next chapter of life. Turn the music up and 2 step your way to it. Remember to hold your head up and smile.
I see you Sis, and I'm oh so proud of you!

Don't Let Your Past Make Your Present Trash

We all make mistakes, it's human nature. Free will. What you did at 16 should by no means reflect on you at 25, 31 or 40+ years of age. Unfortunately, it will because some people will never forget or forgive. Nor do they want to see you do better. Fuck'em! Step from underneath that dark cloud, close the umbrella, and put your shades on. The sun light that will shine on you once you forgive yourself and walk in your purpose will be so bright and clear you might get sunburned…in a good way.

The past paves the way for your future. It's up to you to control your path. Don't let your past make your present trash. What's for you will be if you stay focused and put in the work. Your gift will make room for you! You're a surviver of the strong, a hero for the weak, substance for the less fortunate, and motivation to the procrastinator. Be the voice of reason to those who don't see a way out.

You're more than who you thought you were. You're more than statistics counted you to be.

You're more than who your past groomed you to be.

You are fuck'n fabulous with sauce on the side!

You Are Appreciated

You work your ass off for others and don't get as much as a pat on the back.

You take off work and get a verbal written. You take off from your kids and get labeled unfit.

You take off from your significant other and they feel you're not bringing anything to the table.

You take off from your friends and family and they say, you're acting funny.

I know you're hot under the collar now because this is the total opposite of who you are. You love everybody and want to do what you can to show them just how big your heart is.

Well, let me tell you…appreciate yourself Sis. Yes, ma'am I said it…APPRECIATE YOURSELF.

It's time you start living your life like it's golden. Loving on yourself and patting yourself on the back. Those who appreciate you will join you, and those who don't will disappear. That's a good thing.

Sayonara suckers, it's been real but, I must take care of and love on me.

Girl, They Are Going to Get WTF You Have to Give

"Hi Guys" …nope, nah, nuh-uh, no. As my marketing specialist says "We're not using our YouTube voice. (eyeroll). Don't change who you are just to get in with the masses. Be your true authentic self. I guarantee you, not the fake you (you.0), will go further on your journey and feel good about who you are while doing so.

I remember in my twenties when I worked as a customer service rep, and had to use that phony voice, "Thank you for calling___, this is Ms. Thomas. How may I help you? I know I have a southern drawl, although I'm a Chicagoan true and through. Whew, I would put on my best "YouTube" voice to make the caller feel good about calling the company. I had to sound educated, and speak proper English, while living by "the customer is always right" rule. What genius made that a rule?! I gave that up, became an addictions counselor, and spoke to my clients with a southern drawl. It worked out because, I stepped up and decided to do something I love, something I'm great at, and I can totally be me.

My first book "Check Mate Bitch" …yes you read it right. I was vexed for a split second about adding bitch to the title.

What will people think? I wanted everybody and their mama to be my audience. Well, that didn't last long because, I walk to the beat of my own drum. I unapologetically added BITCH to the title of my first and second book for good measure. Yes, Honey put some stank on it!

Today, I respect those who respect me, and I will pour into those who does the same for me. I'm not a tit for tat person however, my journey is that of growth and the only way I can successfully achieve growth is to A) Focus on self, B) Surround myself with like-minded people who are on my level or higher, and C) Execute the plan.

Yes, I'm acting funny because let's face it, what can I learn from a twenty plus year friend who continues to act like we did back in the 90's. That's right…nothing!

If anybody got a problem with you being true to yourself, look them in the eye's and tell them, take wtf I have to give, or gone nah, I'm busy.

Everywhere You Turn There You Are (Encourage Yourself)

You didn't tell me you love me.

You never support me.

You're supposed to be my friend, but you never support my business.

I did this, that, and a third for them but no one said thank you.

Blah blah blah blah…

Nobody owes you anything. Nobody can care for you like you care for yourself. Nobody's going to love you like you love yourself.

You are everywhere you go, everything you do, everything you see. It's you! You came into this world alone, even if you have a twin, one of you came out first and your DNA will separate you.

Everywhere you turn there you are. You are unique. Thank you for loving you, and supporting you, and being friendly to you, and taking care of you. Thank yourself and encourage yourself.

I know you looked in the mirror after you read this.

Go ahead and brush your shoulder off.

Give yourself two snaps in Z formation and twerk.

Place your crown on your head and say, "Hey Siri, play Golden by Jill Scott".

Dock Your Ships When They No Longer Flow With Your Waves (Relation-Ships, Friend-Ships, Family-Ships, and Situation-Ships)

Say this aloud, "If you're not on my wavelength, please leave this Ship or you will be thrown overboard…Management."

For various reasons people will come and go in and out of your life. Ideally, we hope for longevity in our Ships and that's okay. However, we know nothing lasts forever…shit is temporary.

We must learn to let people, places and things go once we outgrow them. No matter who they are! Holding on to them for convenience, to save face, because they are blood, mud, or water, or whatever foolery you make yourself believe, will only make you exhausted, angry, stressed and depressed. Feelings of loneliness in a room full of people due to a lack of connection. Holding on to Shipwrecks also turns you into a liar because now you're making up shit to turn down invites, phone calls, and text responses.

Situationships will make you Google, "Untraceable substance used to poison someone." (Disclaimer: The above statement is simply for a wow factor. Please don't try this at home, and no I've never truly thought about poisoning anyone...).

In closing, set boundaries for yourself and know that it's A-Okay to release all that is stunting your growth.

Say this aloud, "I'm to grown for this, that, and them. I've outgrown it all. IT'S QUITS".

Mirror, mirror, on the wall they better get in tune or fuck'em all.

To Be The Best Version Of Yourself, You Have To Choose Yourself

I remember being "the toxic one" in the relationship!

Having a man sit there and watch me break down from their actions. I had literally reached a point where I found myself apologizing for my existence and that's when I knew I had lost my light! I saw the craziest side of me, and it broke me. See, they never want to discuss what triggered you, just how you reacted. This version of me wasn't built overnight. This is pain. This is insecurity. This is abuse. This is depression. I HAD to experience all of that to get to who I am today, and I promised myself that I will never get involved with someone that would take me out of my peace like that ever again.

~Anonymous

Don't Dismiss My Feelings

Hey, you, it's me your conscious talking…again. The signs are all there like the ones in the back of the drivers ed booklet. Take heed to them and detour, you'll thank yourself later for avoiding that collision.

People will show you who they are the first time, don't wait on the rerun to play. Simply change the channel to a commercial free station…no interruptions, no repeats.

Stop and think about how you feel and what you need to heal. Take time for yourself before you blackout and can't recover.

Your feelings matter! Don't let anyone convince you that they don't. The offender will try and turn the tables on you and make it all about themselves. Don't fall for it. Stand your ground and use your voice.

(Insert offenders name), it offends/hurts/angers me when you dismiss my feelings. My feelings are valid because they are mine, and you can't tell me how to feel. I deserve to be heard and I will no longer allow you or anyone else to dismiss my feelings on a matter that concerns me.
The most important person in my life is me.

4-6-89...6:02am

His head crowned

She screamed

A black woman coaxed her to push one more time

She screamed

They all cheered, it's a boy

She cried

Feelings of excitement, fear, and loneliness all attacked her at once

Do you want to hold him? A woman's voice could be heard repeatedly, so motherly and soft

Yes, she whispered

Are you ok? Another woman's voice could be heard. Not as caring as the previous woman but concerned, nonetheless.

Yes, she said with attitude

He laid upon her breast

She smiled

He opened his eyes

Her eyes teared

He closed his eyes

She rubbed his cheek with her right index finger

The motherly voice spoke "We must take him for a moment"

She looked afraid

I promise he'll be back the motherly voice assured

"Thank you" She whispered

Is there anyone we can call? The motherly voice asked, placing her hand upon her shoulder…the father maybe?
He's on his way to school
"Your mom?" the motherly voice spoke with soft lines around her eyes
Yes please!
Hello, Ma, it's a boy!
Yes, I'm ok, he looks ok, the lady said he's ok…ok Ma, see you when you get here.
The motherly voice returns even more excited. She speaks, as I said, he's alright
Born 4-6-89 at 6:02 AM, 7lbs,10oz ,21in, 10 fingers and toes, lungs very strong as we all heard.
She smiles, silently prays, and gives her new bouncing baby boy a little squeeze….

That bouncing baby boy is 32 now with his own son
She is me and I am her. I was 16 when he entered the world, excited but afraid,
alone but, had a village on our side.
He was never a hindrance
We made it and we're still making it.
No matter what life brings
Don't give up and don't give in
Solicit those who are rooting for you
You may trip and fall but finish the race

It's doable…

I'm living proof of it!

~ Honey

Tell Somebody

Shout it out, write it out.
Speak bold and clear.
Even if you're afraid.
It's not your fault.
Free yourself.
You're not alone.
Tell somebody.

Confirmation

Confirmation appears in many forms. It's not always a spoken word, text, phone call or telegram.

Confirmation may be a single flower growing in a bed of weeds. A butterfly stopping to enjoy a bed of Coneflowers, or perhaps a hawk stopping by to perch on the tree limb in your front yard.

For every experience extract the good from it and see how you can grow from it. You may fail at some things however, it's not the end-all of your being. Try again and again, as many times as it takes. Don't give up or give in. Your confirmation is calling you to be the best form of you…a WINNER. Winning is in your DNA! All forms of negativity may form in your mind, telling you, you can't. Release those thoughts!

Don't focus on what the past says your family went through, therefore you are destined to follow those steps. Your steps have been ordered and redirected. You are a chain-braker, a generational curse crusher. You can handle all tasks placed before you, with ease.

You are the most important person in your life. Be good to you. It's been confirmed.

That's The Way I Feel About Cha

Once upon a time in '92 a boy walked into my life mesmerized.

He's now a grown man and still in awe of me in '21.

Endless love,

The End.

Issues

If you don't want me then don't talk to me
~Fantasia

He has mommy issues Sis, which is why he can't operate on certain levels without you.

Aw Sis, you have daddy issues which is why you're hanging on.

You both need saving.

Love Won't Let Me Wait

Sometimes I can literally feel my heart breaking. Those are the days I reach out to the ones I love, and who in turn reciprocate the same love back to me. I can literally feel the needle and thread mending my heart back together.

Being fragile is okay if you don't succumb to it. Acknowledge those feelings, seek help, learn and grow from it.

Loving self is a daily necessity. You are a top priority, come out of the shadows and demand the best.

Love won't let you wait to be who you're destined to be. Loving you reminds you that you're worth it. It reminds you that you are number one in a world that may not see you for you, may not like you for you, may not love you for you. But you have an obligation to yourself to love and care for you.

Look in the mirror, growl and repeat, "I'm no punk b*tch, I got this, because I love me."

Be Quiet, Be Still

Every action doesn't need a reaction.
It's ok to just stfu sometimes.
Your peace will thank you later.

Hell-Yeah, I'm Mad

Mad as hell walking around looking like Viola, crying and snoting all over the place.
Throat chakras clogged, feeling strangled. Hair mangled, eyes sweating so bad they're tangled.
All due to a lack of you not standing strong on who you are…I know the feeling.
Makes you want to reach out and touch everybody in reach.

But you're operating out of a different bag today. Your bag is filled with self-love, self-worth, resilience, courage, strength and peace.

Reach in that bag from yester-year and say…And another thing, take all your bullshit back that you unloaded onto me. I didn't ask for it, and you didn't ask if I wanted it…you just left it here.
It's okay to tell people to back up and give you fifty feet. Allow yourself time to ponder on your next move. You owe yourself time to make sure your next move is your best move, and whatever you choose is for your good.

Go ahead and handle that business with no regrets.

Honey

Thick thighs save lives

Red hair is a dare

I've lived, laughed, and loved in my 48 years of life

Phenomenal woman

Wife, Mother, and Grandmother

Risk taker

Heartbreaker

No nonsense

Cuss like a sailor

Dope AF

Lover and Fighter

I'm an Author and Counselor, and I'm serious about my $hit

I'm at peace with SELF

The Good, The Bad, The Ugly

Guilt

Hurt

Shame

Defeat

Anger

Music

Conversations

Old friends

Old lovers

Family

Current friends

Current lovers

Work

Abortion

Money

The minority

The majority

The disenfranchised

The incarcerated

The drug addicted

The terminally ill

Molestation

Fucking Covid19 and all its variations

Suicide

Past

Present

Future

Resentments

Life must continue. You owe it to yourself to continue your journey. Look at the list of words. Whichever word or words resonates with you, (or add your own words) scream it out, followed by "You no longer have jurisdiction in my life, you don't control me, nor do you define me".

Remodel and Rebuild

Ashes to ashes, dust to dust, my happiness in someone else hands I won't in trust.

There comes a time when you must take self-inventory.

If you're not willing to risk the little things in your life going wrong, you'll never get the chance to witness the big things go right.

Let people know, don't come at me about nothing because, I'm shutting down for construction.

Take the necessary time off, to scan yourself from head to toe. Listing the pros and cons. Choosing quality over quantity, self-love over self-hate.

Remodel and rebuild yourself from the top of your head (the way you think), to your heart (the way you feel), to the soles of your feet (the way you move).

Don't come up for air until you know the transformation is complete. There are no more leaks in the building. Square your shoulders and prepare yourself to be the pillars that keep your frame together. You're shining like newly waxed hard wood floors. It's okay to open the window of your heart and share a bit of yourself. However, don't forget to build the privacy fence as well. You must protect your peace.

You're a one-of-a-kind structure, and you're no longer for sale.

Sun Rain Down on Me

A Little Bit of Everything a Whole Lot of Nothing
~ Uncle Dog

Listen up! Your reality will come gliding in your life slicker than a can of oil.

You must always have your antennas up and in a V-shape, to catch the frequency.

Don't fall for the banana in the tailpipe, or the old okey-doke.

Watch out for the one nightstand trying to attach itself to your life dwelling.

It's okay if you fell for the wrong person at the right time in your life. They offered you a little bit of everything and your eyes opened wide, shining brighter than the sun. Then nightfall came and that same light dimmed, once you saw what they offered was a whole lot of nothing.

Now you're having a hard time looking at yourself in the mirror. Praying that the sun continues to shine in your favor. Begging the rain to wash this person away. Crying out sun rain down on me right now with no hesitation.

The rain seems heavy, the sun won't be bright every day, dark clouds are looming. It may seem like the end of a beautiful you. You're wondering how it can be daylight and darkness at the same time.

Just hold on, fight with all your might. Brighter days are ahead. You don't have the luxury to give up, or give in. You are counting on you, you need you, you are capable of any and everything you put your mind, heart, and soul to. You got this.

Now ask the sun to rain down on you in celebration of a job well done. You saved yourself!

Write the Vision Make it Plain
~Scripture

Do you know what you want out of life?

If you answered yes to this question, that's awesome. Most people don't know what they want out of life. Some know they wanted all the toys in the world at 5 years of age.

My own house so I don't have to follow any rules, at 16 years of age. I just want to party and travel at 20+ years of age. OMG these bills at 30+ years of age. I'm tired, but I have goals at 40+ years of age.

Focus. It's never too late to start goal setting or switching gears in your career.

Write down your goals utilizing the SMART system.
Specific…simple and significant.
Measurable…meaningful.
Achievable…attainable.
Relevant…realistic.
Time-bound…time sensitive.

Do you have anyone that you can count on to hold you accountable?

It's okay if you don't. We currently live in a world of apps, notifications and social media groups. Figure out who and what works for you and find something or someone to be an accountability partner.

ACT NOW!

I bet the ideas are swarming in your head. Your journal is currently being filled with ideas. You're probably looking for some old journals from high school when you wanted to be a poet, author, journalist or nurse.

Compare new goals to old goals and commend yourself for any that's been achieved. If it's none, don't fret. Remember it's never too late to start now.

Nothing beats a failure but a try.

Self-Compassion

With love in your heart and fuel in your spirit, have compassion for yourself.

Do you not see what an amazingly dope soul you are?

Do you not feel how deserving you are of love and forgiveness?

Self-compassion is not feeling sorry for yourself. Rather it's being kind to yourself, self-motivation, speaking kindly about yourself, self-encouraging, self-love, and self-care.
I bet you do these things for others, and barely, if at all find the time to do them for yourself.

We sometimes get caught up in pleasing others, and forget we need to show ourselves the same love and respect.

Then we wonder why anxiety, stress, depression, anger, resentments, headaches, neck tension, and so on and so forth sets in.

We must show ourselves compassion. We must say to ourselves, I (insert your name), deserve better than I give myself credit for. I deserve to be kind, gentle and loving to myself. I deserve to request a raise. I deserve a vacation without feeling selfish, hell I deserve to be selfish every now and again.

I know you felt good reading what you deserve because, I felt good writing it.

We deserve to give ourselves a break and provide self-love to ourselves unapologetically.

I'm a nurturer by nature, so this is coming directly from my heart to yours. Be self-compassionate.

Black Lotus Flower

The year was 1957 during the month of July. A beautiful Black Lotus flower sprouted.
Taking its first breath in a world of the unknown. Unaware of its surroundings or what lied ahead.

Fast forward to 1972 sometime during the month of May or June, this beautiful Black Lotus flower sprouted to become a troublesome teen. Hanging out, sneaking around, doing what typical teens do. She met a boy, and they discussed the birds and the bees and things.

Fast forward to 1973 sometime in February, one of the nuns at the school this beautiful Black Lotus flower attended, made a call to her parents. It went something like, "I'm calling to report that your daughter is pregnant." I can only imagine the parent on the other end of the phone leaned against the wall, or perhaps fainted.

March of 1973, a beautiful bouncing Red Lotus was born, and the Black Lotus didn't know what to do. She was only 15 years of age (turned 16 July of that same year) with her entire life ahead of her. She had friends, boyfriend(s), school, siblings, and hard knock parents. Once she came home with the beautiful Red Lotus, her parents took over and watered the Red Lotus as their own. The boy never came around to claim Red Lotus, and Black Lotus never brought up so much as his name to Red Lotus. The Black Lotus couldn't really object to her parents, so she went on with her life adding two more flowers to the garden.

Black Lotus life took a turn and spiraled down a path of weeds, gravel and unhealthy soil. The 1980's came and went with Black Lotus attending school and starting a short-lived career in nursing. The 1990's hit, and she picked up unimaginable vices and made it a career of unhealthy living, bad relationships, trauma, and turmoil. She always meant well, she loved the flowers in her garden however, she just didn't have the rainwater it took to water them properly. Black Lotus life was truly an example of sunny with a chance of rain. When the sun shined on her she was at the top of her game. But somewhere, somehow the dark clouds would always show up and rain on her parade. This cost her more than she was able to bargain for. It tainted her relationships with loved ones.

A dark cloud was cast over her garden and that caused all her flowers, Red Lotus included, to suffer traumatic experiences. Generational curse, after curse, after curse. Red Lotus became an angry, bitter teen, following down some of Black Lotus footsteps. Although Red Lotus didn't live in the garden, she was still apart of it. Cut from the same flower, identical thick roots running through her veins. A stubborn flower growing up way to fast, never stopping to appreciate the sun, moon, stars, or the water that fed her. She took life for granted for many years, feeling that the world owed her for the garden she was planted in. She didn't ask to be here, and surely didn't ask for the problems that came with every breath she took. How fair was that to a young girl? It simply wasn't.

As time moved on, Black Lotus got worse, and Red Lotus got angrier with the world. Despising those who started the main garden, for not protecting her more. Not realizing they did the best they could with what they had to work with. Still and all, they should have tried harder.
Black Lotus had good and bad days…more of them were bad than good. She tried to shield her flowers from the desolate surroundings. Unfortunately, it just wasn't meant to be at that time, and her flowers withered a bit.

The 2000's looked more promising for Black Lotus, she kind of sort of got her garden together. From time to time out of the murky waters she would stick her head up to breathe easy. Red Lotus found her roots and begin to nourish her own garden. Forgetting the days of old and gaining traction on the world ahead. Red Lotus met her dad for the first time in 2007 at the age of 34. Although she thought of him often, she opted out of a relationship with him on the count of his vices. In August of 2021, he took his last breath, and Red Lotus felt a slight void. However, from him she was blessed with a beautiful flower named after a planet.

We know when it seems too good to be true more than likely it is. In 2004, 2008, and 2010, Black Lotus lost her parents and younger brother. She couldn't handle the trauma and again turmoil took over and she was never able to recover. Red Lotus suffered tremendously.

In 2011, Black Lotus lost her battle with the vices of the world. She took her last breath on December 17, 2011. Red Lotus felt as if she took her last breath as well.

In 2021, Cynthia Lynn Thomas (Black Lotus) legacy lives on. Her garden is still blooming fine, with weeds, flowers, bees, butterflies, and things. She has grands and great-grandchildren, and a slew of family who miss her dearly.

Mama you lived your truest life unapologetically. I can hope to live my truest life as well. I hope I'm making you proud.

Love,
Poobie (Red Lotus)

P.S., I have five grandboys and they call me Honey =)

Sunny with a Chance of Rain

Things don't always turn out the way you imagine
Ups and downs are bound to happen
Feelings of stress and depression cloud your judgement
Reckless thoughts and actions step in
Boom, a thunderous sound alters your reality
You're on a downward spiral
Until one day you look up and the overcast is clear
There's no more rain in the clouds
The warmth of the sun startles you
Your eyes lock in with the bright rays
It burns a little, your face softens, your mouth forms an O
A sudden feeling of protection squeezes life in you
Oh Joy
The sound of laughter tickles you
You're reminded that Love was never lost, only hidden,
waiting on you to acknowledge your destiny, your strength,
your worthiness
A butterfly lands on a Lotus Flower
A red cardinal softly sings from a burgundy shrub
Today will be Sunny with a Chance of Rain

Author's Note

Thank you for your support!
Reviews are welcomed and appreciated!

Other Books From this Author:
 Check Mate Bitch!
 Check Mate Bitch! Game Over The Sequel
 Confusion
 The Adventures of Shad and JuJu: Just Because I'm Little Doesn't Mean I Can't Do It

Follow me on all social media platforms:
 Facebook: @author.honeythomas
 Instagram: @author.honeythomas
 Twitter: @redlotusreads
 Website: www.redlotusreads.com

"And one day she decided to pick up a pen and write"
 -Honey Thomas

Honey Thomas is a Chicago, Illinois native. She is an avid reader of urban fiction novels which inspired her to write her first book. The plethora of books, short stories, and poems she has read throughout high school to the present day, allowed her mind to escape into a world of fascination, mystery, realities, and suspense. Being an author allows her to share her creative mind with the world in hopes of giving them the same escape she experienced. Honey is currently working on her next novels.

www.ingramcontent.com/pod-product-compliance
Lightning Source LLC
LaVergne TN
LVHW041550070426
835507LV00011B/1029